I0803341

STUDY GUIDE

Signed, Sealed, Delivered

An Introduction to Covenant Theology

J.V. Fesko

LIGONIER MINISTRIES
Renew your Mind.
LIGONIER.ORG | 800-435-4343

421 Ligonier Court, Sanford, FL 32771
Email: info@ligonier.org

Printed in China.

Contents

Introduction

How does God establish a relationship with us? Throughout history and even eternally, God relates to us through covenants. This reality is at the heart of how we read the Bible and how we understand the saving work of Jesus Christ. In this teaching series, Dr. J.V. Fesko presents the essentials of classical Reformed covenant theology, surveying the overarching covenants of Scripture: the covenant of redemption, the covenant of works, and the covenant of grace. We'll see how God has executed His eternal plan of salvation through the perfect work of Jesus Christ, how He meets us in the sacraments, and how He joins us together as a church—all for His glory.

This study guide is a companion to the video teaching series. Whether you are using the DVDs, streaming the videos on Ligonier.org, or going through the course in Ligonier Connect, this resource is designed to help you make the most of the learning experience. For each message in the series, there is a corresponding lesson in this guide. Here is what you will find in each lesson:

INTRODUCTION	The introduction is a brief paragraph that summarizes the content covered in the lecture and considered in the study guide lesson. **How to use:** Use the introduction to each lesson to get a sense of the big picture before watching the video. Refer to these statements as you work through the study guide to remind yourself of what you have already covered and where you are headed.
LEARNING GOALS	The learning goals are the knowledge and skills that the study guide lesson will endeavor to equip you with as you work through the lecture content. **How to use:** Familiarize yourself with the goals of each lesson before engaging its contents. Keeping the overall purpose in mind as you watch each video and reflect on or discuss the questions will help you get the most out of each lesson.
KEY IDEAS	The key ideas are the major points or takeaways from the lecture. **How to use:** Use these ideas to prepare yourself for each lesson and to review previous lessons. They describe specifically the knowledge that each lecture is communicating.

REFLECTION & DISCUSSION QUESTIONS	The questions are the guided reflection and/or discussion component of the lesson that is intended to help you prepare for, process, and organize what you are learning. **How to use:** Reflect on individually or discuss in a group the questions in the order in which they appear in the lesson. The time stamps in the right margin indicate where the answers to questions during the video can be found.
PRAYER	The prayer section offers suggestions for how to close the lesson in prayer with respect to what was taught in the lecture. **How to use:** Consider using each lesson's prayer section as a guide to personal or group prayer. These sections follow the ACTS prayer model, which you can learn more about in R.C. Sproul's Crucial Questions booklet *Does Prayer Change Things?* This helpful guide is available as a free e-book at Ligonier.org.
REVIEW QUIZ	The review quiz is a set of six multiple-choice questions that appears at the end of each lesson. **How to use:** Use each quiz to check your comprehension and memory of the major points covered in each lecture. It will be most beneficial to your learning if you take a lesson's quiz either sometime between lessons or just before you begin the next lesson in the study guide.
ANSWER KEY	The answer key provides explanations for the reflection and discussion questions and answers to the multiple-choice questions in the review quiz. **How to use:** Use the answer key to check your own answers or when you do not know the answer. Note: Do not give in too quickly; struggling for a few moments to recall an answer reinforces it in your mind.

Study Schedules

The following table suggests four plans for working through the *Signed, Sealed, Delivered* video teaching series and this companion study guide. Whether you are going through this series on your own or with a group, these schedules should help you plan your study path.

	Extended 8-Week Plan	**Standard 6-Week Plan**	**Abbreviated 4-Week Plan**	**Intensive 3-Week Plan**
Week	**Lesson**			
1	*	1	1	1 & 2
2	1	2	2 & 3	3 & 4
3	2	3	4 & 5	5 & 6
4	3	4	6	
5	4	5		
6	5	6		
7	6			
8	*			

* For these weeks, rather than completing lessons, spend your time discussing and praying about your learning goals for the study (the first week) and the most valuable takeaways from the study (the last week).

1

What Is a Covenant?

INTRODUCTION

The culmination of God's covenantal relationship with His people is expressed in terms of a marriage, the marriage between Christ and His church. Covenant theology is the story of this marriage. In this lesson, Dr. Fesko introduces the overarching covenants of classical Reformed covenant theology and defines what exactly is meant by the term *covenant*.

LEARNING GOALS

When you have finished this lesson, you should be able to:

- Describe briefly the covenants of redemption, works, and grace
- Define the term *covenant* and identify the characteristics of a covenant and the types of covenants in Scripture

KEY IDEAS

- The covenant marriage between God and His people is a theme that runs throughout Scripture.
- In its most basic sense, a covenant is an agreement between two or more persons.
- There are seven primary characteristics of the covenants that are found in the Bible.
- In Scripture, we see covenants between the Father, Son, and Holy Spirit; between God and people; and between human beings.

REFLECTION & DISCUSSION QUESTIONS

Before the Video

What Do You Think?

Take a moment to answer the following questions. They will prepare you for the lecture.

- What is your goal in undertaking this study on covenant theology?
- How would you define the term *covenant*?

Scripture Reading

Then I heard what seemed to be the voice of a great multitude, like the roar of many waters and like the sound of mighty peals of thunder, crying out, "Hallelujah! For the Lord our God the Almighty reigns. Let us rejoice and exult and give him the glory, for the marriage of the Lamb has come, and his Bride has made herself ready; it was granted her to clothe herself with fine linen, bright and pure"—for the fine linen is the righteous deeds of the saints.

—Revelation 19:6–8

- In this lesson, we will learn that this passage is steeped in the doctrine of the covenants. What might be the chief purpose of God's covenants, according to this passage?

During the Video

Answer the following questions while you watch the video. They will guide you through the lecture.

The Doctrine of the Covenants Introduced *0:00–6:20*

- How does the end of the Bible connect to its very beginning?
- What covenants are the focus of this teaching series? Briefly describe them.

The Characteristics and Types of Covenants *6:20–22:50*

- How is the term *covenant* defined?

- What are the seven features of biblical covenants?

- What are the three different types of covenants?

After the Video

Answer the following questions after you have finished the lecture. They will help you identify and summarize the major points.

- How does marriage give us a picture of God's covenant relationship to us throughout Scripture?

  If you are in a group, have the members read Hosea 1 and discuss their insights from this passage as it relates to marriage as a picture of God's covenant.

- How does the concept of covenant help us understand the nature of God's promises in the Bible? Consider how this applies to the three covenants that are the focus of this teaching series.

  If you are in a group, have the members name and explain different attributes of God that give them confidence that God is willing and able to keep His promises as expressed through covenants.

- What is a covenant? Provide an answer that incorporates the definition, features, and types of covenants explained in this lecture. What is a danger of being too restrictive in defining *covenant*?

  If you are in a group, have the members identify which of the three covenants they have the most questions or confusion about.

PRAYER

Commit what you have learned from God's Word in this lesson to prayer.

- Praise God for His willingness to create us and enter into a relationship with us.
- Confess ways that your faithfulness has waned though God remains faithful.
- Thank God for covenanting as Father, Son, and Holy Spirit to redeem a people for Himself.
- Ask God to work through His Spirit as you continue to study about covenant theology, that it be not merely informational but transformational.

REVIEW QUIZ

Use these multiple-choice questions to measure what you learned from this lesson.

1. Where does the basic definition of *covenant* in this lecture originate?
   a. The Westminster Shorter Catechism
   b. Luther's Small Catechism
   c. The Heidelberg Catechism
   d. The Children's Catechism

2. How many times does the English word *covenant* appear in the English Standard Version of the Bible?
   a. Less than fifty times
   b. Between fifty and one hundred times
   c. Between two hundred and three hundred times
   d. More than three hundred times

3. The covenant of redemption took place after the fall.
   a. True
   b. False

4. What does the term "cutting a covenant" refer to?
   a. Cleaving to a covenant party through a faith promise
   b. Confirming a covenant through cutting animals in half
   c. Formally agreeing before witnesses through a blood oath
   d. Splitting the terms of the covenant between two parties

5. What idea most relates to God's covenant with Abraham as described in this lecture?
   a. Common grace
   b. Eternal kingship
   c. Self-maledictory oath
   d. Perfect obedience

6. Which of the following is *not* a characteristic of a covenant?
   a. Laws
   b. Oaths
   c. Promises
   d. Ritual washings

Answer Key—What Is a Covenant?

REFLECTION & DISCUSSION QUESTIONS

Before the Video

What Do You Think?

These are personal questions. The answers should be based on your own knowledge and experience.

Scripture Reading

- In this lesson, we will learn that this passage is steeped in the doctrine of the covenants. What might be the chief purpose of God's covenants, according to this passage?

  This passage sings of the great marriage supper of the Lamb. Over the course of this series, we will learn the full significance of its connection with the covenants of Scripture, but on its surface the passage does offer us insight into the ultimate purpose of God's covenants. Words of praise, such as "hallelujah," "rejoice," and "exult," highlight the chief end of God's covenants: that we might "give him the glory."

During the Video

The Doctrine of the Covenants Introduced

- How does the end of the Bible connect to its very beginning?

  The end of the Bible connects to its very beginning through the concept of a marriage covenant. In the beginning, this concept is seen in the marriage of our first parents, Adam and Eve, but their sin introduced death, conflict, and evil into the world. They were even driven out from God's presence. Jesus is the fulfillment of God's promise in Genesis 3:15, and Paul identifies Him as the second Adam (1 Cor. 15:45), the implication being that the church is the second Eve. Connecting the beginning to the end, the marriage supper of the Lamb in Revelation 19 is the culmination of the marriage between Christ and His church.

- What covenants are the focus of this teaching series? Briefly describe them.

  The focus of this teaching series is on the three major covenants of Scripture: the covenant of redemption, the covenant of works, and the covenant of grace. The covenant of redemption is the intra-Trinitarian covenant among the Father, Son, and Holy Spirit. The covenant of works is God's covenant with Adam that was conditioned on his perfect obedience. The covenant of grace is God's gracious provision of salvation for His people despite Adam's failure.

The Characteristics and Types of Covenants

- How is the term *covenant* defined?

  The term covenant *is defined as "an agreement between two or more persons." Isaiah 28:15 helps clarify how "covenant" is interchangeable with "agreement," just as "death" and "Sheol" are interchangeable: "Because you have said, 'We have made a covenant with death, and with Sheol we have an agreement.'"*

- What are the seven features of biblical covenants?

  There are seven important features of the covenants that are found in the Bible. Covenants contain oaths, laws, sacrifices, blessings and curses, love, witnesses, and covenant signs. Each of these features can be found in the various covenants of the Bible to greater and lesser degrees.

- What are the three different types of covenants?

  Three types of covenants that are found in the Bible are God's covenant with Himself as Father, Son, and Holy Spirit, as seen in the covenant of redemption; covenants between God and man, as seen in God's covenants with Adam, Abraham, Noah, Moses, and David; and covenants between people, as seen between Abraham and Abimelech or between Jacob and Laban, for example.

After the Video

- How does marriage give us a picture of God's covenant relationship to us throughout Scripture?

  Marriage *is simply another way of saying* covenant. *The marriage of our first parents opens Scripture, but the introduction of sin, death, and evil into the world needs to be overcome through another marriage, the marriage between God and His people. This marriage is traced throughout Scripture and is seen in God's marriage to Israel at Mount Sinai, in Israel's unfaithfulness as pictured in Hosea, and finally in the covenantal marriage between Christ and the church.*

- How does the concept of covenant help us understand the nature of God's promises in the Bible? Consider how this applies to the three covenants that are the focus of this teaching series.

  Covenants have a promissory character, and they emphasize what God Himself will do. God's promises as expressed through covenants are therefore binding. God binds Himself in His promise to fulfill the terms of our covenant relationship. This is seen in the covenant of redemption and in the covenant of grace, especially when God "cuts" a covenant with Abraham, taking upon Himself the curses of the covenant, the curses that Jesus Christ, in eternity, promised to bear.

- What is a covenant? Provide an answer that incorporates the definition, features, and types of covenants explained in this lecture. What is a danger of being too restrictive in defining *covenant*?

A covenant is an agreement between two or more persons, whether between the persons of God, between God and man, or between people, and often includes oaths, laws, animal sacrifices, blessings and curses, love, witnesses, and signs. While this definition captures every feature that was presented in this lecture, we do not want to be too restrictive in our definition, demanding that every covenant have every feature explicitly present.

REVIEW QUIZ

1. **D.**
   Question and answer 22 of the Children's Catechism is "What is a covenant? An agreement between two or more persons." This definition of covenant *is basic but appropriate because of the difficulty of defining the term.*

2. **D.**
   The term covenant *is difficult to define because it occurs, as an example, 301 times in the popular English Standard Version translation.*

3. **B.**
   The covenant of redemption is an eternal covenant, and though it was made in light of the fall, it was not made after it in time. This eternal covenant was between God the Father, Son, and Holy Spirit to redeem a people for Himself.

4. **B.**
   In Genesis 15, God made a covenant with Abraham. During this covenant-making ceremony, God passed through the cut pieces of animals, as was customary in Abraham's day. Entering into a covenant is described in the language of "cutting a covenant" throughout the Hebrew Bible.

5. **C.**
   God's passing through the animal halves had a very significant point: God was taking upon Himself both the obligations of the covenant and the curses that would come from our breaking the covenant. He was making a "self-maledictory oath." He would fulfill it and take the penalty of our failure upon Himself.

6. **D.**
   Though baptism is a covenant sign that may bring to mind ritual washings, such washings are not a common element in the Bible's covenants, which include oaths, laws, animal sacrifices, blessings and curses, love, witnesses, and signs.

2

The Covenant of Redemption

INTRODUCTION

The covenant of redemption is the eternal covenant made by and between the Father, Son, and Holy Spirit to create and save a people. Some have dismissed the idea of such a covenant as an attempt to divine the mind of God. But this doctrine is biblically sound and necessary. In this lesson, Dr. Fesko outlines the historical origins, scriptural foundation, and basic parameters of the covenant of redemption.

LEARNING GOALS

When you have finished this lesson, you should be able to:

- Understand the meaning and significance of the covenant of redemption
- Trace the development of the doctrine of the covenant of redemption historically
- Support the validity and necessity of the covenant of redemption with Scripture
- Name the requirements and promises of the covenant of redemption

KEY IDEAS

- The covenant of redemption is an eternal agreement within the Trinity to create and save a people.
- The covenant of redemption is confessionally supported, but the primary reason that it ought to be affirmed is that it is supported by Scripture.
- The covenant of redemption serves as the foundation of God the Father, Son, and Holy Spirit's activity in redemptive history.

REFLECTION & DISCUSSION QUESTIONS

Before the Video

What Do You Think?

Take a moment to answer the following questions. They will prepare you for the lecture.

- What is your initial response to the idea of an eternal covenant within the Trinity? What questions do you have?

- What would be some practical implications of the covenant of redemption for the Christian life?

Scripture Reading

When Jesus had spoken these words, he lifted up his eyes to heaven, and said, "Father, the hour has come; glorify your Son that the Son may glorify you, since you have given him authority over all flesh, to give eternal life to all whom you have given him. And this is eternal life, that they know you, the only true God, and Jesus Christ whom you have sent. I glorified you on earth, having accomplished the work that you gave me to do. And now, Father, glorify me in your own presence with the glory that I had with you before the world existed."

—John 17:1–5

- How does this passage work against the idea that the covenant of redemption is a speculative doctrine?

During the Video

Answer the following questions while you watch the video. They will guide you through the lecture.

Historical Origins *0:00–8:46*

- How did the early church fathers and medieval theologians contribute to the understanding of the covenant of redemption?

- What role did the Reformation play in the development of this doctrine?

Scriptural Evidences *8:46–16:08*

- What verses are used to support the concept of the covenant of redemption?

- How does Psalm 110 support the concept of an intra-Trinitarian covenant?

Setting Forth the Doctrine *16:08–23:32*

- What are the three chief requirements of the covenant of redemption?

- What are the six promises of the covenant of redemption?

After the Video

Answer the following questions after you have finished the lecture. They will help you identify and summarize the major points.

- Is the doctrine of the covenant of redemption a product of the Reformation? Why or why not?

  If you are in a group, have the members discuss how studying the historical development of a doctrine is helpful. Ask: Why would it be a fallacy to doubt a doctrine's validity solely on account of its historical development?

- How does Hebrews 7 enhance our understanding of Jesus' role in the covenant of redemption?

  If you are in a group, have the members read the entirety of Hebrews 7. Ask: What makes Jesus' priesthood unique?

- What requirement or promise of the covenant of redemption do you find most surprising and why?

  If you are in a group, have the members share what questions they still have about or related to the covenant of redemption.

PRAYER

Commit what you have learned from God's Word in this lesson to prayer.

- Praise God for His eternal wisdom and plan for our creation and redemption.
- Confess your responsibility for your sin, to magnify the grace of God in sending His Son to pay the penalty for your sin.
- Thank God for the assurance that comes from His eternal covenant of redemption, that He has eternally willed your salvation in Christ.
- Ask God for His Spirit to supply this assurance.

REVIEW QUIZ

Use these multiple-choice questions to measure what you learned from this lesson.

1. Which Reformation pastor and theologian significantly contributed to the articulation of the covenant of redemption in his study of Luke 22:29?
   a. John Calvin
   b. Martin Luther
   c. Theodore Beza
   d. Huldrych Zwingli
2. Which biblical passage indicates that the Father gave the Son a work to accomplish?
   a. Hebrews 7:20–22
   b. John 17:4
   c. Luke 22:29
   d. Psalm 110:1, 4
3. What passage is an intra-Trinitarian conversation about the Son's reign?
   a. Hebrews 7:20–22
   b. John 17:4
   c. Luke 22:29
   d. Psalm 110:1
4. According to Hebrews 7, what role does Jesus fulfill in the covenant of redemption?
   a. A Prophet like Moses
   b. A Priest after the order of Melchizedek
   c. A King in the line of David
   d. A Judge of the people
5. It was not essential for the Son of God to become man to fulfill the requirements of the covenant of redemption.
   a. True
   b. False
6. Which of the following is not one of the six promises within the covenant of redemption?
   a. The Son would be equipped with the Holy Spirit.
   b. The Son would receive the elect as His reward.
   c. The Son would have all authority and power.
   d. The Son would return to His bodiless state.

Answer Key—The Covenant of Redemption

REFLECTION & DISCUSSION QUESTIONS

Before the Video

What Do You Think?

These are personal questions. The answers should be based on your own knowledge and experience.

Scripture Reading

- How does this passage work against the idea that the covenant of redemption is a speculative doctrine?

  Far from a speculative attempt to divine the mind of God in eternity, the doctrine of the covenant of redemption is rooted in Scripture, and it follows logically that God's plan would precede His working in history for our salvation. This perspective is seen in Jesus' words in this passage, that Jesus was "sent," was sent "to give eternal life," and would be glorified as He was "before the world existed" after accomplishing the work given to Him by the Father.

During the Video

Historical Origins

- How did the early church fathers and medieval theologians contribute to the understanding of the covenant of redemption?

  Though the early church fathers and theologians of the Middle Ages did not use the term covenant of redemption, *they understood and taught the substance of the doctrine. They recognized that such passages as John 17:4, which mentions the Father's giving Jesus a work to accomplish, demanded an explanation outside space and time. The Gospels contain no testimony about when the Father called Jesus to this work during His earthly ministry; this call must have been eternal.*

- What role did the Reformation play in the development of this doctrine?

  One of the hallmarks of the sixteenth-century Reformation was the continued emphasis of the Renaissance's ad fontes, *"to the sources." The return to the original Hebrew and Greek texts of the Bible was important. Theodore Beza, exemplifying this conviction, did work in Luke 22:29 from the Greek text, recognizing that it should be understood as "I covenant to you a kingdom as My Father covenanted to Me a kingdom," rather than simply "appoint," as in the King James Version.*

Scriptural Evidences

- What verses are used to support the concept of the covenant of redemption?

  Dr. Fesko referenced the following verses to support the concept of the covenant of redemption from Scripture, in order: Luke 22:29; John 17:4–5; Psalm 110:4; Hebrews 7:20–22; John 5:36–37; John 15:26.

- How does Psalm 110 support the concept of an intra-Trinitarian covenant?

  Psalm 110 supports the concept of an intra-Trinitarian covenant by relating for us a conversation between the Father and the Son: "The LORD says to my Lord: 'Sit at my right hand, until I make your enemies your footstool'" (v. 1). Verse 4 also tells of the Father's appointment of the Son to be a "priest forever after the order of Melchizedek," which Hebrews explains was a covenantal oath (7:21).

Setting Forth the Doctrine

- What are the three chief requirements of the covenant of redemption?

  The three chief requirements of the covenant of redemption are that (1) the Son would assume a human nature; (2) the Son would serve as a Priest on our behalf; and (3) the Son would merit and complete the work of salvation and, with the Father, send forth the Spirit.

- What are the six promises of the covenant of redemption?

  In the covenant of redemption, the Father promised (1) to prepare a body for the Son (Heb. 10:5); (2) to equip the Son with the necessary gifts and the Holy Spirit (Isa. 42:1); (3) to support the Son in His work and deliver Him from death (Ps. 16:10); (4) to reward the Son for His completed work by enabling Him to send out the Spirit (Acts 2:33); (5) to give the Son the elect as His reward (Rev. 7:9); and (6) to reward the Son with all authority and power for the government of His church and the earth (Matt. 28:18–19).

After the Video

- Is the doctrine of the covenant of redemption a product of the Reformation? Why or why not?

  While Reformed theologians, especially in the seventeenth century, began to speak of the intra-Trinitarian covenant of redemption, the doctrine is not strictly a product of the Reformation. A distinctive of the Reformation is sola Scriptura, *"Scripture alone," meaning that the Bible serves as the final authority for faith and life. The doctrine of the covenant of redemption was not produced but rather became more fully articulated through the study of Scripture.*

- How does Hebrews 7 enhance our understanding of Jesus' role in the covenant of redemption?

  Hebrews 7 richly describes Jesus' priesthood, especially the eternal nature of that role and work. He is described as a Priest after the order of Melchizedek, of whom Scripture does not speak about a beginning or an end; Jesus is a Priest "forever." The work He accomplishes as Priest is that of a "guarantor of a better covenant," taking on all the legal obligations of the covenant on our behalf.

- What requirement or promise of the covenant of redemption do you find most surprising and why?

  This question is subjective but requires an understanding of what the requirements and promises of the covenant of redemption are. Dr. Fesko reflected that the most surprising and humbling promise is perhaps that the elect, who are sinners redeemed by grace alone, are Christ's reward.

REVIEW QUIZ

1. **C.**
   Theodore Beza, in comparing the Latin translation of Luke 22:29 to the original Greek text, recognized that Luke had not used the word "to appoint" (as in the KJV) but rather used the word "to covenant." The verse would then be translated "I covenant to you a kingdom as My Father covenanted to Me a kingdom," establishing the idea that the Father covenanted with the Son.

2. **B.**
   In John 17:4, Jesus says, "I glorified you on earth, having accomplished the work that you gave me to do." The following verse might help to contextualize when this work was given: "before the world existed" (v. 5).

3. **D.**
   In Psalm 110, David communicates how the Father directs the Son, "Sit at my right hand, until I make your enemies your footstool," when he says "the LORD says to my Lord" (v. 1). The Father also declares, "You are a priest forever after the order of Melchizedek" (v. 4). The New Testament quotes Psalm 110 more than any other psalm, and it is applied to Jesus Christ. Psalm 110 allows us to listen in on an intra-Trinitarian conversation.

4. **B.**
   Jesus is our great Prophet, Priest, and King, and He will judge the world. Hebrews 7, however, speaks of Jesus' priesthood after the order of Melchizedek. This chapter also names Him as "the guarantor of a better covenant" (v. 22).

5. **B.**
   The first requirement of the covenant of redemption that Dr. Fesko outlined was that the Son would assume a human nature to carry out His covenantal work (Gal. 4:4). He did this so that He would represent us and, being sinless, perfectly so (Heb. 4:15).

6. **D.**

   The first promise of the covenant of redemption that Dr. Fesko outlined was the Father's promise to prepare a body for the Son (Heb. 10:5). There is no promise that the Son, after assuming a human nature, would ever be without a human nature. Westminster Shorter Catechism 21 answers the question "Who is the Redeemer of God's elect?" in this way: "The only Redeemer of God's elect is the Lord Jesus Christ, who, being the eternal Son of God, became man, and so was, and continueth to be, God and man in two distinct natures, and one person, forever."

3

The Covenant of Works

INTRODUCTION

The word *covenant* does not appear in the opening chapters of the Bible. Does this mean that it is mistaken even to begin talking about God's making a covenant with Adam? In this lesson, Dr. Fesko explains why we ought to affirm the reality of the covenant of works by examining its historical origins, scriptural evidence, and theological framework.

LEARNING GOALS

When you have finished this lesson, you should be able to:

- Define the covenant of works and identify its biblical basis
- Explain how the covenant of works is implied in Genesis 1–3, even though the term is not explicitly mentioned
- Recognize the historical development and theological significance of the covenant of works within Reformed theology

KEY IDEAS

- Though the word *covenant* does not appear in Genesis 1–3, the elements of a covenant are present and can be inferred from its context.
- The idea that God covenanted with Adam is confessionally supported and can be proved scripturally with such texts as Hosea 6:7.
- Adam is the federal head or representative of all humanity in the covenant of works; his disobedience affected all his descendants.

REFLECTION & DISCUSSION QUESTIONS

Before the Video

What Do You Think?

Take a moment to answer the following questions. They will prepare you for the lecture.

- What features are typically found in a covenant in the Bible?

- The word *works* is usually set in opposition to the gospel, but how might works relate to the gospel?

Scripture Reading

Therefore, just as sin came into the world through one man, and death through sin, and so death spread to all men because all sinned—for sin indeed was in the world before the law was given, but sin is not counted where there is no law. Yet death reigned from Adam to Moses, even over those whose sinning was not like the transgression of Adam, who was a type of the one who was to come.

—Romans 5:12–14

- How does this passage illustrate Adam's role as our representative?

During the Video

Answer the following questions while you watch the video. They will guide you through the lecture.

Historical Origins 0:00–6:25

- What is the covenant of works?

- In what ways can apocryphal books be used in our study, such as in tracing the development of the doctrine of the covenant of works?

Scriptural Evidences 6:25–16:59

- What features of the covenant are found in Genesis 1–3?

- How do Hosea 6:7 and Romans 5:14 support the idea of a covenant between God and Adam?

Setting Forth the Doctrine *16:59–23:50*

- How can one demonstrate that the blessing of life was offered to Adam for his obedience?
- How does Jesus answer the lawyer's question in Luke 10:25 concerning eternal life? Why is this important?

After the Video

Answer the following questions after you have finished the lecture. They will help you identify and summarize the major points.

- How is God's covenant with Adam pictured in Israel's history?

  If you are in a group, have the members skim Matthew 1–3. Ask: How is Jesus' life a picture of both Adam's and Israel's experience?
- How does Deuteronomy 28–34 work with Genesis 1–3 to bookend the Pentateuch, and what aspects of Israel's law were connected to these opening chapters of Genesis?

  If you are in a group, have the members read the Ten Commandments in Exodus 20:1–21. Ask: What stands out about God's opening words and Israel's response?
- Why is affirming Adam's federal headship important?

  If you are in a group, have the members reflect on Christ's work. Ask: What are the implications for our theology of salvation because Jesus is our federal head?

PRAYER

Commit what you have learned from God's Word in this lesson to prayer.

- Praise God for His holiness, justice, and anger against sin.
- Confess your inability to fulfill the righteous demands of God's law and need for Christ's perfect obedience.

- Thank God for providing Christ as the second Adam, to fulfill the covenant of works where the first Adam failed.
- Ask God for the Spirit's powerful working in you to put sin to death.

REVIEW QUIZ

Use these multiple-choice questions to measure what you learned from this lesson.

1. What is *not* one of the key words describing the obedience required in the definition for the covenant of works?
   a. Partial
   b. Perfect
   c. Perpetual
   d. Personal
2. Which uninspired book was noted to mention the concept of a covenant related to Genesis 2:16–17?
   a. The Didache
   b. The Book of Enoch
   c. The Wisdom of Ben Sirach
   d. The Wisdom of Solomon
3. Which is *not* one of the features of a covenant present in Genesis 1–3?
   a. Covenant signs
   b. Covenant mediator
   c. Covenant blessings and curses
   d. Covenant parties
4. Numerous confessional documents of the seventeenth century, including the Irish Articles of 1615, affirm the covenant of works.
   a. True
   b. False
5. How does Hosea 6:7 support the concept of a covenant in the early chapters of Genesis?
   a. It compares Israel's transgression to that of Adam.
   b. It explicitly mentions the covenant signs of the garden.
   c. It describes the blessings and curses of a covenant.
   d. It refers to the creation directly.
6. What New Testament chapter teaches the federal headship of Adam?
   a. Luke 3
   b. Romans 5
   c. 1 Timothy 2
   d. Jude 14

Answer Key—The Covenant of Works

REFLECTION & DISCUSSION QUESTIONS

Before the Video

What Do You Think?

These are personal questions. The answers should be based on your own knowledge and experience.

Scripture Reading

- How does this passage illustrate Adam's role as our representative?

  This passage teaches how sin and death entered the world through Adam, which indicates that Adam's disobedience had consequences for all humanity. Even though the passage mentions that "all" people sin, it also communicates that Adam's sin was unique and that the sin of others "was not like the transgression of Adam," and Romans 5:19 says that "by the one man's disobedience the many were made sinners."

During the Video

Historical Origins

- What is the covenant of works?

  Dr. Fesko defined the covenant of works as "the first covenant that God made with Adam, wherein He promised him and his offspring eternal life upon the condition of perfect, perpetual, and personal obedience to His commands."

- In what ways can apocryphal books be used in our study, such as in tracing the development of the doctrine of the covenant of works?

  The Wisdom of Ben Sirach is an example of an uninspired, apocryphal book that illuminates for us how people in the intertestamental period interpreted the Old Testament. Because these works are uninspired, they are to be used like any other book, and they can still be helpful if understood as commentaries of the Bible, showing how the Bible was read.

Scriptural Evidences

- What features of the covenant are found in Genesis 1–3?

  Even though the word covenant *does not appear, Genesis 1–3 still has indicators that a covenant was in force with Adam. For one, God's covenantal name appears twenty times in Genesis 2–3. In addition, God gives Adam commands in commissioning him to subdue the earth. God also issues curses when forbidding Adam to eat of the Tree of Knowledge of Good and Evil; he would live if he obeyed and would die if he disobeyed. Furthermore, the trees in the garden, representing life and death, can be understood as signs of the covenant.*

- How do Hosea 6:7 and Romans 5:14 support the idea of a covenant between God and Adam?

  Speaking of Israel, Hosea 6:7 says that "like Adam they transgressed the covenant." Paul also uses a specific word to speak of Adam's "transgression" in Romans 5:14, which elsewhere refers to a covenantal transgression. Paul uses the same word as found in the translation of Hosea 6:7 in the Septuagint, the Greek translation of the Old Testament.

Setting Forth the Doctrine

- How can one demonstrate that the blessing of life was offered to Adam for his obedience?

  An inference has to be made from the penalty—death—that God promises Adam if he eats from the Tree of Knowledge of Good and Evil. The inference is that Adam would have life if he did not eat from the tree. Westminster Confession of Faith 7.2 supports the reality that life was offered to Adam by citing Romans 10:5 and Galatians 3:12, which both communicate that the perfect righteousness of obeying the law would result in life.

- How does Jesus answer the lawyer's question in Luke 10:25 concerning eternal life? Why is this important?

  Jesus answers the lawyer's question, "What shall I do to inherit eternal life?" (Luke 10:25), with another question, "What is written in the Law?" (v. 26). This question reveals that eternal life is the blessing of perfect obedience. Not being able to fulfill the law perfectly, we have to look to the perfect obedience of another—namely, Christ's perfect obedience.

After the Video

- How is God's covenant with Adam pictured in Israel's history?

  God's covenant with Adam is mirrored in Israel's history through the parallels between Adam's experience in the garden and Israel's experience in the promised land. Both Adam and Israel were required to obey God's commands, but both failed, resulting in exile. This parallel between Adam and Israel was a reading strategy of the Pentateuch among rabbis from the fourth to sixth centuries.

- How does Deuteronomy 28–34 work with Genesis 1–3 to bookend the Pentateuch, and what aspects of Israel's law were connected to these opening chapters of Genesis?

  Deuteronomy 28–34 and Genesis 1–3 function as bookends to the Pentateuch by mirroring the themes of blessing and curse, obedience and disobedience, and life and death. Genesis 1–3 details the conditions for life in Eden, while Deuteronomy 28–34 outlines the conditions for life in the promised land. Dr. Fesko also pointed out that specific laws related to Genesis 1–3, the tenth commandment echoing Eve's sin of covetousness and the laws for the priests echoing Adam's commission in the garden to "work it and keep it" (compare Gen. 2:15 and Num. 3:7–8).

- Why is affirming Adam's federal headship important?

  Affirming Adam's federal headship is important because it explains Scripture's teaching about the doctrine of original sin and the necessity of Christ's redemptive work. Adam, as the federal head, represented all humanity in the covenant of works. His disobedience brought sin and death into the world, making us unable to keep the requirements of the covenant of works. Praise be to God, Christ keeps those requirements for us as the new Adam. Christ's work is applied to us through His headship, and if we deny the headship of Adam, then we are in danger of denying the headship of Christ.

REVIEW QUIZ

1. **A.**
   Dr. Fesko defined the covenant of works as "the first covenant that God made with Adam, wherein He promised him and his offspring eternal life upon the condition of perfect, perpetual, and personal obedience to His commands." It required total obedience.

2. **C.**
   The Wisdom of Ben Sirach 14:17 quotes from Genesis 2:16–17, helping us to see how people during the intertestamental period viewed the covenantal nature of God's relationship with Adam: "All flesh waxes old as a garment; for the covenant from the beginning is 'You shall die the death.'"

3. **B.**
   A covenant mediator is necessary now that the covenant of works has been broken by Adam's sin. The promise of a Mediator in Christ can be found in Genesis 3:15, but it is not one of the features common among the covenants in the Bible.

4. **A.**
   While it is lesser known among the confessional material that was released in the seventeenth century, the Irish Articles of 1615 are among those that do affirm the covenant of works. Others include the Westminster Confession of Faith, the Savoy Declaration, and the Second London Baptist Confession of Faith.

5. **A.**
   Hosea 6:7 says, "But like Adam they transgressed the covenant; there they dealt faithlessly with me," which communicates that Israel's covenant transgression can be compared to Adam's sin and that thus Adam was also in covenant with God.

6. **B.**
Romans 5 is the locus classicus *when it comes to demonstrating the federal headship of Adam. The other texts do mention Adam, but they are not sufficient to demonstrate the doctrine. First Corinthians 15:22, however, is also a strong text for demonstrating our relationship to Adam (and to Christ) as our federal head: "For as in Adam all die, so also in Christ shall all be made alive."*

4

The Covenant of Grace

INTRODUCTION

Just as works and grace are in opposition for our justification through God's free gift of faith, so the covenants of works and of grace stand in stark contrast. In this lesson, Dr. Fesko explores the historical origins, biblical evidence, and essential points of the covenant of grace. Through this exploration, we will see how salvation is consistently presented as being by grace alone through faith alone across both the Old and New Testaments.

LEARNING GOALS

When you have finished this lesson, you should be able to:

- Explain the key distinctions between the covenant of works and the covenant of grace
- Identify how the concept of the covenant of grace is evident in both the Old and New Testaments
- Understand the historical development of the covenant of grace and articulate the doctrine

KEY IDEAS

- God sent His Son to faithfully fulfill the obligations of the covenant of works, so that we might be saved.
- Throughout the Bible, salvation has always been by grace alone, through faith alone, in Christ alone.
- The Noahic, Abrahamic, Mosaic, and Davidic covenants and the new covenant are all unfolded as expressions of the one covenant of grace.

REFLECTION & DISCUSSION QUESTIONS

Before the Video

What Do You Think?

Take a moment to answer the following questions. They will prepare you for the lecture.

- How do you perceive the relationship between the Old and New Testaments?
- Was there a way to be saved apart from Christ, even for Israel, before He came? Why or why not?

Scripture Reading

Now it is evident that no one is justified before God by the law, for "The righteous shall live by faith." But the law is not of faith, rather "The one who does them shall live by them."

—Galatians 3:11–12

- How does this passage show the stark contrast between the law and faith?

During the Video

Answer the following questions while you watch the video. They will guide you through the lecture.

Historical Origins *0:00–6:22*

- How did Irenaeus express the substance of the covenant of grace?
- How does the Westminster Confession of Faith express the continuity of the Old and New Testaments?

Scriptural Evidences *6:22–18:48*

- How does the Noahic covenant set the stage for the covenant of grace?
- How do the Abrahamic and Davidic covenants connect?

- Why was the new covenant required?

Setting Forth the Doctrine *18:48–23:18*

- Why is it significant that Jesus is called the "last Adam" in 1 Corinthians 15:45?

After the Video

Answer the following questions after you have finished the lecture. They will help you identify and summarize the major points.

- How is the covenant of grace seen immediately in the garden after the fall?

  If you are in a group, have the members reflect on the grand narrative of Scripture. Ask: How is what you are learning about covenant theology shaping the way you think about the Bible?

- What was the role of the Mosaic covenant within the broader framework of the covenant of grace?

  If you are in a group, have the members reflect together on how the role of the Mosaic covenant might connect to the Christian's relationship to the law.

- Briefly summarize the thread of God's covenant of grace from each covenant after the fall to its ultimate fulfillment in Christ.

  If you are in a group, have the members read Hebrews 11:1–12:2. Ask: How is the covenantal continuity of the Old and New Testaments expressed by the letter's author?

PRAYER

Commit what you have learned from God's Word in this lesson to prayer.

- Praise God for His unchanging nature as seen in His covenant promises and fulfillment.
- Confess any ways that you boast in your works and the pride of self-righteousness that is antithetical to the covenant of grace.
- Thank God that, in His Son, He has provided a righteousness that we could not have achieved.
- Ask God for a deeper humility by the Spirit concerning His gracious provision of Christ for you.

REVIEW QUIZ

Use these multiple-choice questions to measure what you learned from this lesson.

1. Which theologian obscured the unity of the covenants?
   a. Heinrich Bullinger
   b. Irenaeus
   c. Marcion
   d. Huldrych Zwingli

2. What is *not* affirmed by the Westminster Confession of Faith concerning the covenant of grace?
   a. There is one covenant of grace throughout the Old and New Testaments.
   b. Under the Old Testament, the covenant of grace was administered to foreshadow Christ.
   c. Under the Old Testament, believers were saved in a different manner than in the New Testament.
   d. In the New Testament, Christ, the substance of the covenant of grace, is revealed.

3. How did Adam demonstrate faith after the fall?
   a. By confessing his sin to God
   b. By leaving the garden of Eden
   c. By sacrificing an animal to cover his sin
   d. By naming his wife *Eve*, "the mother of all living"

4. God changed the requirements of the covenant of works after it could no longer be maintained.
   a. True
   b. False

5. According to Galatians 3, why was the Mosaic covenant added?
   a. To prevent idolatry
   b. Because of transgressions
   c. To restate the covenant of works
   d. Because of the insufficiency of the unconditional covenants

6. What was Dr. Fesko's biggest takeaway regarding the covenant of grace?
   a. The covenant of grace is the covenant in which Christ does the work for us.
   b. The covenant of grace replaces the need for any form of obedience or response.
   c. The covenant of grace ensures that those who follow God's law closely will have eternal life.
   d. The covenant of grace focuses on the importance of faith but requires continual acts of obedience to complete the work of salvation.

Answer Key—The Covenant of Grace

REFLECTION & DISCUSSION QUESTIONS

Before the Video

What Do You Think?

These are personal questions. The answers should be based on your own knowledge and experience.

Scripture Reading

- How does this passage show the stark contrast between the law and faith?

  Scripture is clear that no one can be justified through the law, for no one in Adam has ever been able to perfectly fulfill the law. This passage contrasts the law and faith and argues that justification is not by law keeping. First, quoting from Habakkuk 2:4, Paul teaches us that the just are those who live by faith. Second, he tells us that the law is not of faith. Therefore, the justified are not made so through the law.

During the Video

Historical Origins

- How did Irenaeus express the substance of the covenant of grace?

  Irenaeus argued against Marcion's false teaching that divided the Scriptures. Marcion taught that the wrath of God of the Old Testament is not compatible with the graciousness seen in Jesus Christ to the point that he preached that there are, in fact, two gods in the Bible. Irenaeus expressed the substance of the covenant of grace by showing the continuity of the Old and New Testaments, arguing that there is only one God and plan of salvation throughout Scripture.

- How does the Westminster Confession of Faith express the continuity of the Old and New Testaments?

  Westminster Confession of Faith 7.5 states that from the Old Testament to the New Testament, there is one covenant of grace, with the Old Testament foreshadowing Christ in its promises, prophecies, sacrifices, and signs. Section 7.5 of the confession further states that the saints of the Old Testament were saved by looking forward to Christ, such that both Old and New Testament believers equally look to Christ alone for salvation (see 7.6).

Scriptural Evidences

- How does the Noahic covenant set the stage for the covenant of grace?

  The Noahic covenant sets the stage for the covenant of grace through God's promise to preserve the world, ensuring that His redemptive plan would continue to unfold. The Noahic covenant is therefore the foundation on which all the subsequent covenants are built.

- How do the Abrahamic and Davidic covenants connect?

  The Abrahamic covenant includes the promise that Abraham would be the father of many nations and that kings would come from him. This promise is further realized and developed in God's covenant with King David. In the Davidic covenant, God promises that David's heir would have an everlasting throne, which points to Christ, the ultimate fulfillment of the promise given to Abraham that all nations would be blessed through his Seed.

- Why was the new covenant required?

  The new covenant was required because Israel failed to keep the Mosaic covenant. Dr. Fesko highlighted the uniqueness of the Mosaic covenant in this regard, that it could be broken in ways that the Abrahamic and Davidic covenants could not. Nevertheless, it was still part of the one covenant of grace.

Setting Forth the Doctrine

- Why is it significant that Jesus is called the "last Adam" in 1 Corinthians 15:45?

  Jesus is called the "last Adam" because He fulfills and completes the work that the first Adam failed to accomplish. This title emphasizes the redemptive work of Christ as central to the covenant of grace. Whereas Adam disobeyed and brought sin into the world, Jesus, through His obedience, secures eternal life for His people. He not only fulfills the covenant of works by living a perfect life but also pays the penalty for the broken covenant.

After the Video

- How is the covenant of grace seen immediately in the garden after the fall?

  The covenant of grace is first seen in Genesis 3:15, where God promises a Redeemer who will come through the Seed of the woman. Despite Adam's disobedience, God's response is not merely judgment but a promise of salvation. We can see the role of faith coming to prominence in Adam's calling "his wife's name Eve, because she was the mother of all living" (Gen. 3:20), a belief in God's promise. God further demonstrates His graciousness by providing garments to cover Adam and Eve's nakedness.

- What was the role of the Mosaic covenant within the broader framework of the covenant of grace?

  The Mosaic covenant was given as part of the covenant of grace but had a specific role: it was "added because of transgressions" to preserve Israel as a people until the coming of Christ (Gal. 3:19). It was intended to preserve Israel from the pagan influence of the surrounding nations to ensure the preservation of the Seed of the woman. It was also to show Israel the impossibility of achieving righteousness through the law.

- Briefly summarize the thread of God's covenant of grace from each covenant after the fall to its ultimate fulfillment in Christ.

  As a summary, your answer will emphasize different features of the history of redemption but should include the beginning of the covenant of grace with the promise of Genesis 3:15 and the covenants with Noah, Abraham, Moses, and David and the promise of the new covenant. Each of these covenants builds on the previous one, progressively unfolding redemptive history.

REVIEW QUIZ

1. **C.**
   Marcion was a second-century heretic who taught that there are two gods, the god of the Old Testament and the god of the New Testament. Such a belief even led Marcion to reject portions of the New Testament. Irenaeus argued against Marcionism by showing the unity of the covenants, which Marcion obscured and denied.

2. **C.**
   Because the covenant of grace spans both the Old and New Testaments, people in both times were saved by grace alone. This salvation was by faith alone in Christ alone. All the rites and ceremonies of the Old Testament foreshadowed Christ, so when believers of the Old Testament put their faith in God's promise to forgive their sins, their faith was fundamentally in Christ.

3. **D.**
   After the fall, God gave the first promise of the gospel that salvation would come through the Seed of the woman. There was still hope for the eternal life that had been lost in the covenant of works. Adam professed faith in this hope by naming his wife Eve, *"the mother of all living" (Gen. 3:20).*

4. **B.**
   God did not change the requirements of the covenant of works but introduced the covenant of grace in which another would fulfill the obligations of the covenant of works on our behalf, making salvation by God's free grace.

5. **B.**
   In Galatians 3:19, Paul writes: "Why then the law? It was added because of transgressions, until the offspring should come to whom the promise had been made." Dr. Fesko described the law's role in preserving Israel and in teaching Israel the impossibility of perfectly keeping it.

6. **A.**
   Dr. Fesko concluded: "The biggest thing that we could walk away with regarding the covenant of grace is that Christ does the work for us, and He pays the penalty for us so that we can enjoy the blessings of eternal life."

5

Covenant Signs

INTRODUCTION

God communicates to our five senses. He communicates to our ears through His Word, and He communicates to our sight, touch, smell, and taste through His covenant signs. In this lesson, Dr. Fesko looks at the significance of God's covenant signs and sacraments throughout biblical history and explains the transition from the Old Testament sign of circumcision to the New Testament sacrament of baptism.

LEARNING GOALS

When you have finished this lesson, you should be able to:

- Identify the covenant signs of the Old and New Testaments and their significance
- Explain the continuity between circumcision and baptism as covenant signs
- Understand how baptism and the Lord's Supper function as means of grace

KEY IDEAS

- Covenant signs—such as the trees of the garden of Eden, the rainbow, circumcision, and the Sabbath—serve as physical, visible representations of God's promises to His people.
- Circumcision was a sign of a regenerate heart (Deut. 10:16) and a sign of the covenantal judgment of being cut off from the people of God.
- Christ's work of being cut off on behalf of His people and of pouring out the Holy Spirit marked the transition from circumcision to baptism.

REFLECTION & DISCUSSION QUESTIONS

Before the Video

What Do You Think?

Take a moment to answer the following questions. They will prepare you for the lecture.

- What did your baptism mean? How is it still meaningful to you?

- Why do we need the sacraments of baptism and the Lord's Supper?

Scripture Reading

In him also you were circumcised with a circumcision made without hands, by putting off the body of the flesh, by the circumcision of Christ, having been buried with him in baptism, in which you were also raised with him through faith in the powerful working of God, who raised him from the dead. And you, who were dead in your trespasses and the uncircumcision of your flesh, God made alive together with him, having forgiven us all our trespasses, by canceling the record of debt that stood against us with its legal demands. This he set aside, nailing it to the cross.

—Colossians 2:11–14

- What does Paul mean by "the circumcision of Christ"?

During the Video

Answer the following questions while you watch the video. They will guide you through the lecture.

Covenant Signs in the Old Testament *0:00–11:35*

- What did the trees in the garden represent?

- What does the rainbow of the Noahic covenant represent?

- How did the Sabbath function as a sign of the Mosaic covenant?

The Transition from Circumcision to Baptism *11:35–22:32*

- What did circumcision represent?

- How does Christ's work relate to the sign of circumcision?

After the Video

Answer the following questions after you have finished the lecture. They will help you identify and summarize the major points.

- How do the Old Testament signs find their fulfillment in Christ, and what implication does that fulfillment have for the signs in the New Testament?

  If you are in a group, have the members reflect on the simplicity of the signs in the New Testament compared to the signs of the Old. Ask: Which more greatly resonates with you and why?

- How does baptism connect to the Holy Spirit and judgment?

  If you are in a group, have the members discuss baptism's meaning on an individual level (see WCF 28.1).

- What is the relationship between the preaching of the Word and the administration of the sacraments?

  If you are in a group, have the members read Romans 10:14–17. Ask: Should the sacraments ever be separated from the preaching of God's Word? Why or why not?

PRAYER

Commit what you have learned from God's Word in this lesson to prayer.

- Praise God for the culmination of His promises in Christ.
- Confess any neglect of God's covenantal signs in your observance of the sacraments of baptism and the Lord's Supper.
- Thank God that He communicates clearly to you, in both your body and your soul, through Word and sacrament.
- Ask God to increase your sense of wonder in your union with Christ as signaled by the signs of baptism and the Lord's Supper.

REVIEW QUIZ

Use these multiple-choice questions to measure what you learned from this lesson.

1. According to Dr. Fesko, what did the tree of knowledge symbolize?
   a. Death
   b. Life
   c. Law
   d. Christ
2. What term is best associated with the rainbow as a sign, as described by Dr. Fesko?
   a. Flood
   b. Human depravity
   c. Future judgment
   d. Warrior
3. What was the sign of the Davidic covenant?
   a. David's throne
   b. Solomon's temple
   c. The Davidic line itself
   d. None of the above
4. What is one difference between circumcision and baptism as covenant signs?
   a. Circumcision is physical, while baptism is purely spiritual.
   b. Baptism is neither bloody nor painful, unlike circumcision.
   c. Circumcision was replaced by baptism, being fulfilled by Christ.
   d. Circumcision and baptism are identical in meaning and practice.
5. The Word does not replace our need for the sacraments.
   a. True
   b. False
6. What does Peter associate with baptism in 1 Peter 3?
   a. Circumcision
   b. Christ's crucifixion
   c. Jesus' burial and resurrection
   d. Noah's ark and the flood

Answer Key—Covenant Signs

REFLECTION & DISCUSSION QUESTIONS

Before the Video

What Do You Think?

These are personal questions. The answers should be based on your own knowledge and experience.

Scripture Reading

- What does Paul mean by "the circumcision of Christ"?

  This passage from Paul's letter to the Colossians closely connects circumcision and baptism, and it helps us understand why the transition from circumcision to baptism as a covenant sign occurred. The context of Paul's phrase "the circumcision of Christ" (Col. 2:11) tells us that it is referring to His bloody death by crucifixion. The phrase is followed by mention of Christ's burial and resurrection.

During the Video

Covenant Signs in the Old Testament

- What did the trees in the garden represent?

  Both the trees in the garden of Eden were signs of the covenant of works. Dr. Fesko argued that the tree of knowledge was the visible sign of God's law, taking as an example Psalm 19:7–8, where God's law is described as "making wise the simple" and "enlightening the eyes." This same language is used of the tree of knowledge in Genesis 3.

- What does the rainbow of the Noahic covenant represent?

  Most fundamentally, the rainbow was a sign of God's promise to never again flood the earth, but there is deeper symbolism in the rainbow itself. The rainbow is an image of a warrior's bow that has been set down so that, reserving His righteous judgment, God brings about salvation by His grace.

- How did the Sabbath function as a sign of the Mosaic covenant?

  The Sabbath functioned as a visible and physical reminder of God's covenant with Israel, symbolizing God's presence among the people and His work in sanctifying them: "Above all you shall keep my Sabbaths, for this is a sign between me and you throughout your generations, that you may know that I, the LORD, sanctify you" (Ex. 31:13). This time of worshipful rest was in anticipation of the eternal rest to come.

The Transition from Circumcision to Baptism

- What did circumcision represent?

  Circumcision was the sign of God's covenant with Abraham, and as the sign of that covenant, it represented the need for a regenerate heart (Deut. 10:16) and pointed to the fulfillment of God's promise of the Seed of the woman.

- How does Christ's work relate to the sign of circumcision?

  Related closely to circumcision as a sign of God's promised Seed, Jesus, who was the culmination of that promise, would suffer the covenant curse, which was taken on by God Himself in the Abrahamic covenant. The sign of circumcision came with a warning: "Any uncircumcised male who is not circumcised in the flesh of his foreskin shall be cut off from his people; he has broken my covenant" (Gen. 17:14). Jesus, in His crucifixion, suffered this "cutting off" on behalf of His people (Col. 2:11–12).

After the Video

- How do the Old Testament signs find their fulfillment in Christ, and what implication does that fulfillment have for the signs in the New Testament?

  Connections can be made from each one of the Old Testament's covenant signs to their fulfillment in Christ. Each one of them pointed to Christ. Found in Christ is eternal life and the Word of God in the flesh, as related to the trees of the garden. Christ is the culmination of the redemptive history that is played out on the stage of the Noahic covenant. Circumcision, the Sabbath, and the Davidic line find their fulfillment in Jesus. These covenant signs terminate in Him as the substance, making way for simpler signs of baptism and the Lord's Supper, which He instituted.

- How does baptism connect to the Holy Spirit and judgment?

  John the Baptist said that Jesus would baptize with "the Holy Spirit and fire" (Matt. 3:11). This baptism of the Holy Spirit and fire came on the day of Pentecost (Acts 2:33). Dr. Fesko made an argument connecting Peter's associating baptism with the Old Testament flood and the outpouring of the Spirit and judgment (1 Peter 3:18–22; 2 Peter 3:5–6; see also John 15:7–11). Just as Noah and his family passed through the judgment waters of the flood, so too do we, in Christ, pass through the flood of the Spirit to salvation rather than judgment.

- What is the relationship between the preaching of the Word and the administration of the sacraments?

  God's Word goes together with His covenant signs. When joined with the preaching of God's Word, baptism and the Lord's Supper act as a seal and confirm God's covenant promises in Christ. We hear God's Word, and we get to experience the sacraments with all our other senses, but they are made intelligible to us by God's Word.

REVIEW QUIZ

1. **C.**
   In Psalm 19, God's law is described as "making wise the simple" and as "enlightening the eyes" (vv. 7–8). This is also how Moses described the tree of knowledge: "the woman saw that the tree was good for food, and that it was a delight to the eyes, and that the tree was to be desired to make one wise" (Gen. 3:6).

2. **D.**
   Each of these concepts can be associated with the flood, but the rainbow was argued to represent God's warrior bow that is hung up in peace, symbolic of God's promise to never again flood the earth.

3. **C.**
   Explicitly, the Davidic covenant did not have a sign as all the other covenants did, but implicitly, its sign is the Davidic line itself. Israel would see the confirmation of this covenant in the Davidic king. Jesus Himself is that sign, the King who reigns forever.

4. **B.**
   Dr. Fesko made points to avoid certain language about baptism and circumcision. Circumcision was not merely physical, nor did baptism replace circumcision. As covenant signs under the one covenant of grace, they both point to the accomplishment of the person and work of Christ. Baptism, however, is not bloody or painful like circumcision, among other differences.

5. **A.**
   We need both the Word of God and the sacraments, for God gave us both. We need the Word to hear God's promise to us confirmed, but we also need the sacraments as means of God's grace.

6. **D.**
   In 1 Peter 3, Peter connects baptism with the Old Testament flood. Noah was brought safely through the judgment waters of the flood by the ark, and we are brought safely through the judgment of baptism, a judgment that Jesus underwent on our behalf.

6

Covenant & Church

INTRODUCTION

While it is true that God saves Christians individually, God covenants with a people and joins us together as a covenant community. This goes against any individualistic approach to our relationship to the church. In this lesson, Dr. Fesko connects covenant theology with the church, focusing on what it means to read the Bible, profess the faith, and live out the Christian life as a covenant community.

LEARNING GOALS

When you have finished this lesson, you should be able to:

- Explain the importance of reading Scripture within the covenant community rather than individualistically
- Understand why creeds and confessions ought to guide our profession of faith
- Think about the Christian life from a covenantal perspective, with a focus on vows, accountability, and discipline

KEY IDEAS

- There are no private interpretations of Scripture but only an understanding that has been established by the church throughout the ages.
- Creeds and confessions help us profess the same faith.
- Living the Christian life requires participation in the covenant community, holding one another accountable to the rule of God's law.

REFLECTION & DISCUSSION QUESTIONS

Before the Video

What Do You Think?

Take a moment to answer the following questions. They will prepare you for the lecture.

- Why is it important for the church to be united in its profession of faith?
- Is accountability and church discipline necessary? Why or why not?

Scripture Reading

And all the people gathered as one man into the square before the Water Gate. And they told Ezra the scribe to bring the Book of the Law of Moses that the Lord had commanded Israel. So Ezra the priest brought the Law before the assembly, both men and women and all who could understand what they heard, on the first day of the seventh month. And he read from it facing the square before the Water Gate from early morning until midday, in the presence of the men and the women and those who could understand. And the ears of all the people were attentive to the Book of the Law. . . . [Others] helped the people to understand the Law, while the people remained in their places. They read from the book, from the Law of God, clearly, and they gave the sense, so that the people understood the reading.

—Nehemiah 8:1–3, 7–8

- How does this passage communicate the importance of reading Scripture in community?

During the Video

Answer the following questions while you watch the video. They will guide you through the lecture.

Reading the Bible as a Covenant Community *0:00–8:36*

- What are some biblical examples of Scripture's being read in a covenant community?
- What is the role of the Holy Spirit in reading Scripture?

Professing the Faith with the Covenant Community *8:36–11:52*

- What passages of Scripture show the importance of having a unified profession of faith?

- What tools does the church have to ensure that we profess the same faith?

Living the Christian Life within the Covenant Community *11:52–22:39*

- Why is church membership fundamental for living the Christian life covenantally?

- What is formal church discipline patterned on? How does it differ from that pattern?

After the Video

Answer the following questions after you have finished the lecture. They will help you identify and summarize the major points.

- What is the difference between God's law as a covenant and God's law as a rule?

  If you are in a group, have the members discuss the role of the law in the Christian life. Ask: How can understanding God's law as a rule rather than as a covenant keep us from legalism in the Christian life?

- What is the goal of church discipline? How can we avoid formal church discipline?

  If you are in a group, have the members discuss why people might have negative views of the church or church discipline. Ask: How can we seek to overcome these issues?

- Describe the most important thing not to forget about the doctrine of the covenant and the church.

  If you are in a group, have the members discuss the most impactful ideas they encountered in this teaching series.

PRAYER

Commit what you have learned from God's Word in this lesson to prayer.

- Praise God for Christ's purchasing the church with His own blood (Acts 20:28).
- Confess ways that you tend toward individualism in relation to your local church.
- Thank God for Christ's gifts to the church and the Spirit's work in helping us understand Scripture.
- Ask God to help you love others with the same covenant love with which He has loved you.

REVIEW QUIZ

Use these multiple-choice questions to measure what you learned from this lesson.

1. Which biblical example illustrates the danger of the private interpretation of Scripture?
   a. Moses' receiving the law on Mount Sinai
   b. The Ethiopian eunuch's reading Isaiah
   c. Eve's exchange with the serpent in Eden
   d. Paul's conversion on the road to Damascus

2. Which most closely describes the role of the Holy Spirit in reading Scripture within a covenantal framework?
   a. Solely inspiring the writing of Scripture
   b. Providing new revelations that replace the written Word
   c. Guiding individual interpretation apart from the church
   d. Assisting the church in understanding God's Word

3. Which term refers to the church's collective understanding of the Scriptures?
   a. *Lex credendi*
   b. *Regula fidei*
   c. *Sola Scriptura*
   d. *Traditio veritatis*

4. What is a function of the law for believers?
   a. As a covenant of works
   b. As a means of justification
   c. As a rule for the Christian life
   d. As a way of condemning others

5. *Christian individualism* is an oxymoron.
   a. True
   b. False

6. Which of the following is *not* a purpose of church discipline?
   a. Restoration
   b. Repentance
   c. Punishment for sin
   d. None of the above

Answer Key—Covenant & Church

REFLECTION & DISCUSSION QUESTIONS

Before the Video

What Do You Think?

These are personal questions. The answers should be based on your own knowledge and experience.

Scripture Reading

- How does this passage communicate the importance of reading Scripture in community?

  In this important moment in redemptive history, Ezra reads the law to the exiles who had returned to Jerusalem and who were about to renew God's covenant with them. The reading of the law, however, was not done without interpretation, which can be given only by some form of community, whether it be with the church currently or historically.

During the Video

Reading the Bible as a Covenant Community

- What are some biblical examples of Scripture's being read in a covenant community?

  Some examples that Dr. Fesko gave were Ezra's reading of the law to the returned exiles in Nehemiah 8 and the Ethiopian eunuch's receiving interpretation of the book of Isaiah from Philip in Acts 8. Both show the importance of reading Scripture in community and provide a proper balance to the private interpretation of Scripture that we might pride ourselves on in our individualistic age.

- What is the role of the Holy Spirit in reading Scripture?

  First, the Holy Spirit has inspired the inerrant Word of God and is the One who stirs our hearts and writes it on them, helping us to understand and remember it, just as Jesus promised His disciples in John 14:26 and 15:26. In pouring out the Spirit, Jesus gave gifts to the church, including pastors and teachers, who are gifted by the Spirit to help us understand Scripture, that the church may be built up (Eph. 4:11–12).

Professing the Faith with the Covenant Community

- What passages of Scripture show the importance of having a unified profession of faith?

  In Galatians, Paul warns the church against accepting any gospel contrary to the one originally preached, pronouncing "anathema" or accursedness on false teachers (1:8–9). Jude 3 calls us to "contend for the faith that was once for all delivered to the saints." Both passages highlight the reality that there is a standard of teaching and one faith to profess in the church.

- What tools does the church have to ensure that we profess the same faith?

  Dr. Fesko named specific creeds and confessions that can be used as tools so that we might profess the same faith. Among the creedal ecumenical councils, he named the Council of Nicaea, the Council of Constantinople, the Council of Ephesus, and the Council of Chalcedon. Among Reformed confessional standards, he named the Three Forms of Unity and the Westminster Standards.

Living the Christian Life within the Covenant Community

- Why is church membership fundamental for living the Christian life covenantally?

  The vows of church membership provide the foundation of our accountability to the church. It is through church membership that we give our consent to be held accountable for our doctrine and life.

- What is formal church discipline patterned on? How does it differ from that pattern?

  Formal church discipline is patterned after the Old Testament covenantal patterns as seen in the various penalties that were imposed for sin, including exclusion from the covenant community and even execution for a capital offense. In the new covenant, however, physical punishment is replaced with spiritual discipline, such as being barred from the Lord's Supper or being excommunicated.

After the Video

- What is the difference between God's law as a covenant and God's law as a rule?

  There is a standard by which we hold our lives accountable to the church, and it is the law of God. But we do not relate to God's law as if it were a covenant. Westminster Confession of Faith 19.6 distinguishes the difference between the law as a covenant and the law as a rule. The law as a covenant demands the perfect, personal, and perpetual obedience that was required of Adam. We cannot fulfill the law as a covenant; it drives us to Christ as we recognize how we fall short of the law's demands. The law also has a positive function in the Christian life: it is our norm or rule for righteous living.

- What is the goal of church discipline? How can we avoid formal church discipline?

  The goal of church discipline is not punishment but repentance and restoration. It is an expression of the Father's love to discipline His children. Living the Christian life in community helps us avoid church discipline; it provides us with discipleship, mutual accountability, and support. As the church, we are called to stir one another up to good works (Heb. 10:24–25) and pick each other up when we fall (Eccl. 4:9; see also Gal. 6:1–2). We cannot fulfill these dimensions of the Christian life without community.

- Describe the most important thing not to forget about the doctrine of the covenant and the church.

  Dr. Fesko identified the most important thing not to forget about the doctrine of the covenant and the church: love colors everything from first to last. Covenant theology is fundamentally rooted in love—God's love originating in the covenant of redemption, in calling Adam to loving obedience in the covenant of works, in sending forth His Son in the covenant of grace despite our sin, and within the covenant of grace, in uniting us into a loving covenant family.

REVIEW QUIZ

1. **C.**
   Eve's exchange with the serpent in Genesis 3 is a prime example of the danger of private interpretation. Even though the serpent twisted God's words, Eve followed his lead and interpreted them according to her own understanding.

2. **D.**
   The Spirit does more than inspire the Word, but in inspiring the Word, who better to explain it to us? Among Christ's gifts to the church are the pastors and teachers who, by the Spirit, teach us the Word of God so that we might become mature in the faith (Eph. 4:11–13).

3. **B.**
   The ecumenical councils of the church have given us the regula fidei, *the "rule of faith," which is the church's collective understanding of the teaching of Scripture. It is the teaching of Scripture that the church has universally professed.*

4. **C.**
   The law has multiple functions. Among the options, only its function as a rule for the Christian life is valid. It is not a means of justification as if it were a covenant of works, nor is it a way of condemning others, although we can use it for spiritual judgment. Dr. Fesko talked about the function of the law in showing us our sin, driving us to Christ, and providing us with a rule for what is pleasing to God in the Christian life.

5. **A.**
Dr. Fesko identified individualism as one of the great challenges to a proper view of the church. God unites us together as Christians into the church, so Christian individualism *is a contradiction in terms. We are called to live out the Christian life within the community of the church, rather than in isolation.*

6. **C.**
Discipline is an act of love aimed at the repentance and restoration of a sinner. The goal of church discipline is not to punish, but to manifest the love of the Father in disciplining the children that He loves when they stray in sin.